Random Thoughts, Limericks, Lyrics, and Dots

Heartache to Humor

Michael L. Beebe Sr.

ISBN 979-8-89309-375-9 (Paperback)
ISBN 979-8-89309-376-6 (Digital)

Covenant Books
11661 Hwy 707
Murrells Inlet, SC 29576
www.covenantbooks.com

Dedicated to my first love and late wife, Michele,
for fifty-six years as my friend, wife, mother, and
grandmother. Michele passed on April 22, 2020.
To Debra Muckel, my best friend and ardent fan.
To Ken and Linda Weyand for putting all my scribble into print.
To my many friends for all their support and
giving me the confidence to move forward.
To Covenant Books for having faith in me and
making the process run smoothly.
Thank you!

Heartache to Humor

February 13, 2021

Butterfly

Friendship is like a butterfly fluttering in the wind.

If you are lucky enough it lands on your rose.

You get to enjoy its beauty until it flutters off.

When all else is gone, you still have the memory of that beautiful butterfly.

Thank you for landing on my rose, my friend.

February 19, 2021

Friendships

Friendships—they come, they go, never knowing the seeds they sow.

How often do we ignore those seeds? A smile, a gesture, a tear shed for someone dear or maybe dead!

A hug, a kiss, they will be missed; true friendships do endure. They last; they mature. They grow year by year.

What is it we fear of having a friendship dear? For they spread across this vast expanse. Friendship is but our only chance.

When we are dead and friendships gone, our memories for a short time carry on.

Be nice, be good, treat each other as though their last day! Don't be the one who said, "I meant to say I love you!" "I'll miss you!" "Please come again!"

Carry on! Carry on!

Life is short, a memory sweet, but friendships are forevermore.

Carry on! Carry on!

February 21, 2021

Dreaming

I dream of the future. I dream of the past. My dreams seem so real; why don't they last?

They are so vivid, so amazing, and surreal. Why do I have them? Maybe just to help me heal.

My dreams waft away like fog in the morning sun, leaving me in doubt. What did I dream? What was it about?

What do my dreams mean? Are they omens of the future? Are they just a visit from a loved one passed? Or are they spells, spells that do not last?

Maybe just sharing a wonderful moment together or sharing a hug, sharing a kiss, seeing my love again, a love that I dearly miss.

Slowly I awake, remembering as I lay, but my dream starts wafting, wafting away.

No more can I hug her or kiss her, it seems.

I can only look forward to another night's dreams. Please don't wake me! Let me dream! Let me dream!

March 2, 2021

Wokeness: Evil and Hate

You were born into this world with true innocence. What could be more innocent than a newborn baby?

All the love taught was for naught. For soon the evil that had been hidden was no longer, no longer forbidden.

Our hearts told us it was wrong, but evil kept singing, singing its song.

Listen to me! Sing my song! Those people you hear, they are wrong! Hate those people for they are wrong! Sing with me; sing my song.

Kick those people; knock them down! Beat them; defeat them; don't let them up! They are in their place; they are wrong! Keep them there; look at their faces; look at their races.

Hate those people! Sing my song, for the people you fear, they are wrong.

Hate those people; sing my song. You are right; they are wrong! You are right; they are wrong.

Hate them; hate them! Sing my song. You are right; they are wrong!

April 18, 2021

Blue-Eyed Lady

I met a lady with big, blue eyes. How they sparkle and hypnotize. Hers not showing, as if unsure how her eyes did allure.

Her smile so radiant and large as life sets off the beauty of those big, blue eyes.

When she talks about a life now past, those tears well up but do not last.

One by one, those tears did drop. Maybe a hug might make them stop.

She's thinking back of all those years—the hurt, the pain, all those lies that could not rob her of those big blue eyes.

I see a young girl with a radiant smile—so much life, so much hope for a little while. Alas, the pain and wonder whys could not rob her of those big, blue eyes.

April 19, 2021

Life Eternal, Heaven, or Hell

It's such a short life! I wonder what's beyond. Is it heaven, or is it hell?

Does our soul tarry on, or does it leave? Does it stay, making sure that a loved one's heart is healed before being called away?

How many days, months, or maybe even years does it take to dry one's tears?

Who has been there and then come back to let us know what we lack?

Were we bad? Were we good? Maybe we were just misunderstood?

Who can know? Who can tell? Are we going to heaven or going to hell?

I tell you, my friends, time will tell. We are going to heaven or going to hell!

Treasures

The loves we have had, the loves we have lost—they are treasures and should be shared at any cost!

Tell us, tell us true, all the loves you've had and those you knew!

Tell us the stories of days gone by, of the hardships, heroics, the history we have missed.

Tell us about the loves you've had and the girls that you've kissed.

Tell us, tell us please, about your life, your loves! Please tell us all! Tell us all. Just don't tease! Leave nothing out. Tell us your stories. Tell them all!

What is love? What is life? If we don't share the treasures hid, who is left to tell what we did and unfold the many stories told?

Tell them all, and please be bold. Leave nothing out, not a thing untold. For your stories, they are gold!

Some won't care, and by all measures, the stories you tell are all your treasures!

April 22, 2021

My Angel

Michele, the love of my life, has passed away a year ago this very day.

The heartache I feel is here to stay.

It will be with me until my dying day.

Everyone says, "With time it will get better." It brings back memories of the first time I met her.

I couldn't believe how stunning she looked.

The halo and aura around her so bright. I would think of her both day and night.

I think back and see her angelic face.

So young, so beautiful. To me, she was the prettiest girl in the human race.

Some would say I was prejudiced, and that's for sure. She had the most beautiful blue eyes and was so sweet and pure.

Michele was so giving; she had a heart of gold,

Taking all of our needs and putting hers on hold.

It didn't matter the time of day, if at work or if at play.

She would be there with a smile, maybe to listen to a friend or just to sit with them for a while.

Even when sick or having a bad day, she would listen to what you had to say.

She was an enabler. She spoiled us rotten. I will never let her be forgotten.

I love you, Michele. I miss you so much. Oh, how I miss your caressing touch on the back of my thumb when holding hands, on the back of my neck to soothe the pain, or just sitting together while we watched the rain.

A gentle kiss upon my lips, my cheeks you so lovingly caressed, and both of us saying, "We are so blessed."

I believe I have been touched by angels, and some won't believe that they showed me things and were here to help me grieve.

The angels are gone now, leaving nary a sign, knowing their job is done, and I will be fine.

Michele, I know you are gone but not far away. We will be together on another day.

We will hug; we will kiss; we will play. I miss you, my angel... until another day.

May 3, 2021

Freedom

Freedom is such a precious thing! What happened to let freedom ring or of thee I sing?

There are people bent on destroying our way of life and all of our dreams!

They do not work and don't have to, or so it seems.

They just lie back. You need not money; this is the land of milk and honey!

What an embarrassment to our veterans, who had fought for their rights, willingly giving it their all, some giving their lives!

What brave men! What brave warriors! Giving it all for these socialist voyeurs as they can only watch, scream, and shout, "Give me more money! My stimulus ran out! Just issue more checks, and print more money! Don't you know? We live in the land of milk and honey!"

If you have become disillusioned, we think we might have found a good solution! You can go home. It's your lucky day. And here is one more thing you don't have to pay because dumping garbage, although not free, is a gift to you from our country; 'tis of thee! We will pack you a lunch and send you on your way! "Hope you go far. Have a nice day! You tried to destroy heaven! I hope you enjoy hell! Good luck. With that, I wish you well!"

What a shame! You had your chance! You thought being here was all song and dance!

Those heroes, who were wounded and died in vain—what did they really attain?

Take your choice of a new location, just don't make the US your destination! "You are losers we can do without. For when you leave, we will scream and shout!"

God bless America, of thee I sing. God bless America; let freedom ring!

May 9, 2021

Spirits

Ethereal spirits—they are surreal! They surround us! They astound us! Open your minds; they are all around us. You have to listen; you have to feel! Pay attention, for they are real!

Don't be afraid; they will not hurt you. They are not here to judge your virtue!

They might scare you; they might alarm you. They are here but not to harm you!

They show you marvelous things that are so real, for their purpose is just to heal, to ease the pain and the heartache that you feel.

They are not here to make demands, only to give us their helping hands!

They come to help to ease the pain. They show us things but not in vain!

For these things, they are subtle and shown to you in different ways to help you through your lonely days.

They show us things that explain so much, but still we miss our loved one's touch!

We miss the warmth, that giving heart, that beautiful smile, the hugs, and the kisses.

And for a while, we wonder if the spirits have gone, leaving no more a subtle sign, as if to say our job is done. You will be just fine!

I heard a door close! I wonder.

May 15, 2021

Memoriam

Emotions shift to and fro, like the ocean's tide that we can't control.

Tears running down my cheek, puddling on the ground at my feet.

I dare not look nor make a sound. But look I do, then I turn around.

Did they see me crying, missing her,

Someone I loved, who is no longer here?

Will they understand?

Will they feel my loss?

Will they feel my heartache or know my thoughts?

Would they see the love we had or the life we shared?

Will they know how much I really cared?

They say time heals but don't say how long.

I can't imagine; I think they are wrong.

When all is done and the last hand shaken and all the hugs and pictures taken, they will all go home, wishing me well.

I'll go back home to my living hell!

May 21, 2021

Angels

The day Eve tempted Adam, the angels decried! For they knew our innocence was gone, and then they cried.

They told us why. They told us when. They told us how.And it began!

It was not evolution that started the human race. It was God's touch and His son giving us grace!

God sent His angels to protect His Son because He knew He was the only one who could save us from our sins. And so the story… it begins.

Some people doubt it! Some people tout it! But still you may ask, Why did He love us? Why did He care?

He gave us faith that we could share! He gives us hope that we were not lost! He would save us, save us at any cost!

The angels watched; the angels cried. They were not to intervene when He was crucified.

He was tortured beyond belief, put on the cross between a robber and a thief!

As God held His angels at bay, He watched His Son die on the cross that day.

He gave His all! He gave his life! With His blood dripping off his feet, He would not let Satan win with all his lies and deceit.

The angels' tears running down their faces knew Jesus Christ just saved the human race.

Was it all worth the suffering and pain? Or did Jesus Christ die in vain?

The angels are here. They watch us. They walk among us> They ask, "Was it justified?"

Are these sinners the reason Christ Jesus was crucified?

And the angels cried.

May 25, 2021

Whiskey

When I drink whiskey, I feel so smart. I know all the answers and where to start!

You can't tell me I've had too much, and drinking whiskey is just a crutch!

I don't think there is a question that I can't answer! Another drink, and I become a very good dancer! Give me another, and I become quite a romancer!

I like whiskey; it's my martini. But to tell the truth, I really like whiskey. and I hate vermouth! You can give me vodka; you can give me gin! But I like whiskey, for it's my old friend!

I know whiskey doesn't hug, and whiskey doesn't cuddle, and there is no answer in the bottom of its bottle!

But for a little while, it helps you forget the love you miss. I would give it up for one last kiss!

May 26, 2021

Masks and Rants

The socialist left insist we wear our masks! To what purpose? you may ask.

They say, "For goodness sake, you will get the virus! Put your mask on. Don't dispute it! You're un-American if you refute it."

Doesn't matter if the science doesn't support it. Wear your mask, or the socialist left will report it! "Put your mask on! We know what's best. Do what we tell you, as we can attest!"

The socialist left follows like sheep. They don't question their leaders and are told things they must not repeat!

"Put your mask on. Don't ask questions!" What a shame; you can't even make suggestions.

Listen to Dr. Fauci, as he knows what's best! He changes his mind daily or just makes a guess! What a joke, and you can't deny; he gives us reason to wonder why.

He gives us reasons to ask, W.H.O. instructs him?

Listen to your heart; use your head! What's the real reason so many are dead?

The socialist left is out to destroy us! They say put your mask on; please come join us. It's almost over! It's almost done! We did all this without one gun!

Think about it. You decide. Was it the Wuhan virus, or was it genocide?

June 5, 2021

Growing Old

When we grow old, we joined the fold of the winners and the losers.

We made our choices; we were so bold!

We didn't think we would ever grow old.

Our youth is slipping away, hour by hour, day by day.

Precious seconds ticking away.

We have lost all of our hopes, all of our dreams, and all of our joy, or so it seems.

All of our losses, all of our gains have been replaced by aches and pains.

Every day that we survive, we count our blessings; we are still alive.

When did our pimples turn into wrinkles?

When did our hair turn gray?

What year was it?

What was the day?

What? Can't hear you! What did you say?

So many things we took for granted.

Our beautiful children, our wonderful friends—

Will we see them tomorrow? It all depends.

No one knows when our life ends!

Our memory is slipping more every day.

But we remember our youth as if it was yesterday.

When did we grow old?

June 12, 2021

Going Home

Heartache is something that has no cure; it can stay with you for years and years.

I feel as though I will never find love again.

I feel my life is over, coming to an end.

I feel it's time for me to go home.

That's where I need to be: I with her, she with me.

I cannot stand the heartache. I cannot stand the pain. Why am I still here?

What is there to gain?

My heart is broken. I feel it's beyond repair.

I live my life in a state of despair.

My days are so lonely without her; my nights are even worse.

Why couldn't I have been the one to die first?

What could be worse than living your life alone, knowing the love of your life will never again come home?

I can't wait to be with her. I don't want to be alone. I want to see her. I want to go home.

June 23, 2021

Healing

I am so lonesome since losing my wife.

My world is so different; it has changed my life.

Now I have to love her and adore her from afar.

What am I to do now?

How do I wear this scar?

How do I show it?

Do I put it on display?

Do I hide it and keep it for yet another day?

Do I show it along with all my many tears?

Is it worthy to show for all of our many years?

What if I would have traveled the road not taken?

Would my faith in God have been forsaken?

Would the love of my life still be alive?

Would she have been diagnosed sooner and maybe survive?

When does healing start? When does it end?

When does my heart finally start to mend?

There are no times. There are no seasons. There are no explanations nor good reasons.

It's just a part of life you can't deny.

You just accept it, and then you die.

June 24, 2021

That's Life

When we were born, some were given a rose; some were given a thorn.

We had no idea of what our life would bring.

Would we cry, or would we sing?

We had so many dreams. We had so much hope. Most of that got washed away by a big bar of soap.

It was like dirt behind the ears; we wore it for years and years.

As we grew older, we became bolder. We would sneak a kiss with rarely a miss and sometimes just got a smile.

But sometimes… well, let's just say, it took us a while.

We found our loves surrounded by turtle doves, flying our hearts away.

They caught us; they had us. What can I say?

Some of us said, what were we thinking?

Can you tell us, were we sober, or were we drinking?

There are no doubts we had our screams and shouts all through the years of our marriage.

But one thing for sure, we loved all of those fights. We wouldn't trade anything for those making-up nights,

With all those hugs and all those kisses.

Life was good again with me and the missus.

June 30, 2021

Glory Train

This old train we are riding, it just keeps chugging, chugging along.

Day and night, we ride it, making many choices, some being right, some being wrong.

Like life itself, we ride it to the very end, never knowing what is next, be it a hill or be it a bend.

We keep wondering, How many miles?

How much longer?

Will riding this train take us up yonder?

We went to the left. We went to the right.

We are riding this train with no end in sight.

Unlike our hearts, with the warmth that we feel, there are miles upon miles of tracks made of cold, cold steel.

We hear a whistle blowing.

Are we slowing down?

It is not our stop yet; it is just another town.

When this train goes by its last station, we better be sure of our salvation!

We ride together for miles and miles, sharing our laughs and those beautiful smiles.

We travel through life with a one-way ticket.

Our ride will end one day; we know not when, nor can we pick it.

Just make sure, when you get on board, you live a good life, for there are great rewards.

This train travels daily, and many will ride.

We all make our choices; some we would like to hide!

It's a long, long journey to our final destination.

Believe in God, and enjoy the celebration!

July 5, 2021

A New Life

My new life's journey has started; it is so full of change.

It is so lonesome, and it is so very strange.

The road so long; I must walk by myself.

I walk this road alone, just me and nobody else.

What will I find if I walk it to the end?

Will I find happiness?

Will I find a new friend?

Am I condemned to loneliness, to a life of despair?

What of my past life? Do I just leave it here?

When will I be able to leave this life for another one new?

What will the future bring me? What will I do?

I must move forward and never look back.

What do I offer? There is so much that I lack.

I can no longer offer my youth, not even good looks.

And might end up traveling or just reading good books.

But one thing is for certain, I will not waste away!

There is so much life ahead and always another day.

I have so much apprehension; I have so much fear.

But one thing is for sure, my new life is starting, starting right here.

July 7, 2021

The Man in the Mirror

I just looked at the man in the mirror and saw someone I hated.

He thought being nice and being good were things so overrated.

He tried controlling his wife; I think he broke her spirit.

He said "I'm sorry" so often; she no longer wanted to hear it.

Her heart so big and damaged, maybe it was broken due to the shouting and all the harsh words spoken.

By the time that he realized, the damage had been done.

He couldn't have hurt her more if he had shot her with a gun.

For so many years, she took his abuse in stride, and for just as many years, she took his abuse and cried.

Over and over, she kept caving, knowing their marriage was well worth saving.

Out of the blue, he made her a promise, that he would be honest and never hurt her again.

He said, "Forgive me. I'll prove it! I'll show you! I know I can!"

His frown turned into a smile; his face picked up a grin,

As she opened up her heart to let him come back in again.

I know what she went through for all of those years; I can only imagine the tears and the tears.

That man I hated, he is long gone. He's no longer here, for now when I look, there is a new man in the mirror.

August 17, 2021

I Just Can't Remember

Have I ever been there? I don't think I have. I just can't remember!

Maybe I will stop and just take a peek. I'm sure it can't wait until early next week!

It's a good question, and it makes me ponder. Is it here, or is it up yonder? I don't know. It really makes me wonder?

If I had been there, was it September, maybe October, or was it November? It might have been the month of December! I just can't remember!

Was I young, or was I old? Was it warm, or was it cold? Did I wear my winter coat?

Did I go by car, or did I go by boat?

I just can't remember!

Did I go by myself, or did I go with a friend? Did I go straight or go around that bend?

I just can't remember!

If you will excuse me as there are some gaps. I'm not sure, and I have no maps.

Do I turn left, or do I turn right? We might have to stop and spend the night!

By the way, who are you? I think I know, but I just can't remember!

August 18, 2021

The Wallet

I was walking the other day, my mind so far away.

I looked down at my feet, dreaming about the girl I would like to meet.

To my surprise, there laid a wallet. It was so different, but I didn't know what else to call it.

I opened it to see what was inside. It had not a penny but a picture. Oh, what a find!

It was the prettiest girl that I had ever seen. It matched the girl who was in my dream.

I look around, and to my surprise, it was that pretty girl and such beautiful eyes!

I waved at her to get her attention. She was so beautiful, or did I mention?

I walked toward her, my heart beating out of my chest. I said I found this wallet. Is it yours? I attest.

She said, It is mine. I dropped it on purpose. You are the man of my dreams. How long I have been looking. Forever it seems!

What are the odds to have crossed the same path? And to find a new love, you do the math!

August 21, 2021

Just One More Kiss

As I sit and reminisce, thinking of our last kiss, I know not where to start, as a teardrop falls upon my heart.

If only I could have had just one more kiss!

The tender touch of her soft lips, her beautiful blue eyes—they mesmerized, and how they hypnotized.

If only I could have had just one more kiss! I would have circled the earth, walking for miles for just one of her beautiful smiles.

If only I could have had just one more kiss! I miss the tender moments, putting my arms around her, squeezing, loving her, caressing her.

If only I could've had just one more kiss! Lonesomeness is now my enemy. It's devouring me; it never leaves! I've never had a hurt, hurt like this!

If only I could have had just one more kiss! I miss the smell of her perfume, so intoxicating every time she entered or left a room. I dream of her most every night, my pillow wet from all my tears, dreaming of all those wonderful years.

If only I could've had just one more kiss! She is gone now. Oh, how I miss her. If she were here, I would surely kiss her.

If only I could have had *just one more kiss!*

August 24, 2021

To the Rear

I met a man who seemed so nice and looked so kind. I said, Sir, if you don't mind, would you watch me walk and judge my behind? Please tell the truth of what you find!

My friend, he said, it would be an honor. But if my wife finds out, I will be a goner!

I said to all of my questions would you please answer and make suggestions?

When I wiggle, does it jiggle? Did you laugh, or did you giggle? When I pounce, does it bounce? Should I squeeze my cheeks? I have been working on them for weeks and weeks.

. How does it look when I get it shaking? Or is that a mistake that I would be making?

He said, Please don't think me mean, but there are some things that should be hidden and never seen!

He said, Please, my friend, I am being kind. Take a look in the mirror at your behind. Even with good intentions and all the new inventions, you can't fix what's in that reflection. And I hope I'm done with this inspection!

I told him, Thank you! You have been so kind for taking the time to judge my behind. I just needed a change in my life. And now I must go home and tell my wife, this was not the answer. Maybe she should apply for that job of pole dancer?

September 24, 2021

Just Do It!

I walk for exercise; I walk most every day. My doctor says to do it now; it's something you can't delay.

He says it's something that cannot wait; it's something I need to do now and not to hesitate.

I walk around a local lake. It's three miles, give or take.

The doctor is right; I feel so good. I gave him a call, and he said, "I knew you would."

He said, Keep up the good work, but try to go faster but not too fast. You might fall, and it would be a disaster.

My breathing became easier and wasn't such a chore. I lost a few pounds, but the doctor wanted more.

The doctor said, "Hold your stomach in, and work on that core. It will get easier, and you won't be so sore."

I get up in the morning. My feet are aching, and my calves are on fire. I can't take a step as I've lost my desire.

I called my doctor. And while he was still talking, I hung up the phone and said, "If it wasn't for him, I would still be walking."

So please take my advice. Walk at your own pace. It's not a competition, and it's not a race.

Just do it!

September 25, 2021

Life Is Good

Every morning, I wake up at six, and breakfast I fix, always me eggs and me bacon.

If ever I changed, it would be sorta strange. And, oh, what a mistake I'd be makin'.

I have a spoonful of flax, and sit and relax with a hot cup of coffee and cream.

What a great life, for I have no strife, except for one small problem, it would seem.

Much to me consternation, I have a little constipation. It's quite a problem, you see.

I have tried every cure, and that's for sure, but nothing seems to work for me.

Try as I may, and try as I might. I tried all day and most of the night.

I called the doctor, he said to bend over, put me head between my knees, and to tickle me nose to make me sneeze.

I followed his instructions to a tee. I felt something move and said, Well, I'll be.

The doctor was right; the end was in sight and all of my problems behind me.

Ah, life is good again!

October 7, 2021

Ashes to Ashes

My heart died the day the love of my life passed away. Only my soul is alive, living day to day.

I await the day, the day of my own demise. I know not when, but it will be no surprise.

I know I will soon be gone, to sleep the sleep of the dead, to no longer have fear, to no longer have dread.

I will finally be at peace, having no more heartache, with no more tears. The pain will be gone, the pain that I have lived with for all these many years.

Misery will no longer gnaw at me, consuming me forever it seems. I will soon be free to enjoy eternity and all of my dreams.

My loves ashes, and those of my own will soon be together and lovingly sown.

Into the wind or back to the earth, I know not if it makes a difference, nor if either be worse.

I know that life is a blessing, and maybe death is no curse. Yet living this life, I can't hurt much worse.

Do not mourn for me. Do not cry nor any sorrow, for we are all born into the world. We live, then we die, and then comes tomorrow.

October 8, 2021

A Man's Work Is Never Done!

My wife did so much that she wore me out. I said, If you need help, just give me a shout!

It was her that made my clothes wearable. It was her that made my life bearable.

It was her who cut my hair. She told me to get it cut, or you're not going anywhere!

It was her who did our laundry, as well as the sewing. She left the yard for me to be mowing.

It was her who did all the cooking, as well as the baking. She left the yard for me to be raking.

It was her who did the dusting. She said the dust was just disgusting!

It was her who vacuumed the floor. I said, Watching you really makes me ache! It's almost more than I can take!

It was her who cleaned the toilets and made the beds, as well as the ironing. She wore me out; it was all so tiring.

I said, Take yourself a break. It would be best! After my nap, you can do the rest!

December 15, 2021

Gone Fishing (Two for One)

Oh, my goodness, I am under so much stress. I'm so tired, for I don't get no rest.

I think I will go fishing! It has been sometime since I threw in a line, and it's a beautiful big trout that I be a wishing.

I bait me hook and take me a look to see where I will cast. I have a feeling, when I get to reeling, that it certainly won't be me last.

'Tis cold in the air and more than I can bear. I am glad I have me bottle. A nip or two is all I will do, any more and I would be a wobble.

Oh there, it is, me beautiful fish a tugging at me line. Just one more nip or maybe two, and I am sure that I will be just fine.

I set me hook and take a look, and to my surprise, I have caught not one, but I have caught two. They are right before me eyes.

I take a nip no more than two just to celebrate me catch. As I reel them in and take a nip again, it's me head that I begin to scratch. For as I looked down, I began to frown, seeing just one fish a dangling.

It was such a puzzle that I had me a guzzle. And glory be to the joys of angling, there were again two fish on the end of me hook, and they were there just a dangling.

Fishing is so relaxing and so much fun but not without me bottle, for I always catch two and never just one after a nip from me bottle.

December 16, 2021

A Real Mulligan

I have good news, Laddy! And what might that be, Paddy? I have met me a lass, and it be a love I cannot hide. I am in love and wish to make her me bride.

Ah! And where might she be from, Paddy? Are ye daft, Laddy? She be a fine Irish lass, one I could not pass. She be full of spunk and of course, red hair. I must find her a gift to show how much I care. Oh, I see, Paddy.

I have good news, Laddy! And what might that be, Paddy? I have bought her a dog! It be a fine dog, Laddy, but it has only three legs. Ah! And what kind of dog might it be, Paddy? Are ye daft, Laddy? It be an Irish setter. Ah! But, Paddy, why only three legs? Laddy, do ye think it might upset her? You know, I only just met her! Oh, probably not, Paddy.

I have good news, Laddy! Ah, what might it be, Paddy? Me future bride made me a stew, Laddy! Ah, and what kind of stew might it be, Paddy? Are ye daft, Laddy? It be an Irish stew with vegetables from her garden, although it be lacking a few.

Paddy, might it have potatoes and carrots, celery and beef? Are you daft, Laddy? Well, no, it didn't, but she not be making me her best! Ye know, after I get to know her, I might be getting the rest. Oh! Now I see, Paddy! She didn't like the three-legged dog. Are ye daft, Paddy?

December 25, 1021

All in Due Time

It is a new day. With a smile, I greet it. I say my morning prayer and then head on. I meet the challenge, come what may.

I treasure this day; it is yet another chance to meet a new friend or a new companion or maybe even romance, but all in due time!

This day is a gift, once spent, will never be lived again. I am in no hurry. I will find a new love but all in due time.

This new day I live, and all that is in me, is there to give, be it a new friend or a new love, but all in due time.

I will know it when I find that special person. I will know it in my heart. I will know it from the beginning. I will know it from the start. It will happen but all in due time.

I know they will be loving. I know they will be kind. They are someone I am looking for and someone I will find but all in due time.

Shall I not look anymore? Should I just let fate open its door? I say, yes, it will happen but all in due time.

December 26, 2021

Exchanging Gifts

I have bad news, Laddy. Ah! And what would that be, Paddy? I have received a gift for Christmas, 'tis the most horrible gift! I know not what to do for sure. Ah! Paddy, what kinda gift is it that would be such a bother and give ye such a stir?

It be a cat, Laddy. It be a shedding, shedding all of its fur! It be full of fleas. And worse than that, Laddy, it be makin' me sneeze. Ah! I see, Paddy.

Could ye not take it to the pound, Paddy? Tell them ye found it just running around.

Are ye daft, Laddy? It be a gift from me bride! If she found out, I would surely be makin' me bed outside.

I need some time to think, Laddy, and some time to ponder. I'm a going home and will be just up yonder.

Laddy! Laddy! I have such good news! Ah! And what would that be, Paddy? The cat was for ye, Laddy! For me, Paddy? Aye, and I got a new pair of shoes, and a fine pair of shoes they be!

Laddy, is it not wonderful news? What do ye think? Its fur is so beautiful and soft as a mink. Nary a flea, not one in sight!

What do ye think, Laddy? Will ye be taking it home tonight?

Are you daft, Paddy?

December 27, 2021

My Old Friends—
Bless Their Soles!

My old walking shoes are showing their age and don't walk near as fast as the latest rage.

But I will take them any day over a new shoe. They have walked many miles since they were bought new.

They have frayed shoelaces and worn to one side. They provide the gait that age cannot hide.

They have holes in their soles, showing miles of use. They are no longer tight and are now kind of lose.

The smell that permeates way past your nose is a reminder not to bring them to close.

I can't let them go, as they are like an old friend; you can't just discard them when it's close to the end.

I will wear them to work, and like an old friend, we will support each other to the very end.

January 2, 2022

The COVID

Laddy, I be having bad news! Oh, what would that be, Paddy? I'm a thinking I be a having the COVID, Laddy. I'm a need to tell someone, and it's ye that I choose.

Oh, I'm so honored, Paddy! But what makes ye think it be the COVID, Paddy? Are ye daft, Laddy? Can ye not see I be a ailing? Every breath is harder, Laddy. I know I be a failing!

Do ye have any other ailments, Paddy? Are ye daft, Laddy? Can ye not see I be a shivering?

Me body is a tremble, and ye can surely see it a quivering! Oh, yes, I see, Paddy. But do ye have a fever or maybe a headache?

Are ye daft, Laddy? Can ye not see me head is twice its size, and it be a throbbing, a throbbing in me eyes? Oh, yes, I see, Paddy, but this is not new to ye. I think what Ye have is called the Guinness flu.

Are ye daft, Laddy? Well, I did stop for one and maybe it be two. Me memory is returning, and maybe it be true. It might not be the COVID that I be having, but I really cannot be sure. I will go back to the pub tonight and see if I can find the cure.

Are ye daft, Paddy?

January 14, 2022

Coffee Mate (Irish Style)

"Oh, I love me coffee. I have it every day. 'Tis something I love, but I will have it only one way. I drink it black with a cap full o' whiskey, no sugar, no cream. It opens me eyes, or so it would seem."

"I cannot go a day without it, and that is for sure. That beautiful, wonderful bean is good for what ails you and, with a cap full o' whiskey, is maybe even a cure."

"Me bride, she drinks her coffee but in another way." "She makes her coffee a chocolate mocha latte."

"I don't be understanding what she be a thinking, but it's the black coffee I be a drinking, without that cup full o' whiskey, it would simply be uncouth. I would not lie, for I simply be tellin' the truth."

"If ye don't like it, then have it your own way. But for me, it's black coffee, a cap full o' whiskey, and I bid you good day!"

January 15, 2022

Colleen

Laddy! I have such good news for ye! Oh! What would that be, Paddy?

I have found ye a Colleen with beauty the likes ye have never seen!

Gorgeous red hair and blue eyes, the color of the sky on a beautiful spring morning!

She be a spunky one, this Colleen! So ye better be careful...just a warning!

Now, Paddy, ye have seen this Colleen with your own two eyes, and it was not just a picture?

Are ye daft, Laddy! Of course, I seen her with me own two eyes. And oh! My goodness, what a prize!

And where would this have been, Paddy?

Laddy, I be telling the truth! It was at the pub named Gilley. And, oh! What a beauty! Oh, what a filly!

Paddy, did ye get her name? Are ye daft, Laddy? Of course I got her name. But ye know, Laddy, after a pint or two... well, she was... was someone kind of new, and her name has slipped me mind! But really, Laddy, she be one of a kind! And did I tell ye, Laddy? Oh! She can surely sing!

Is she married, Paddy? Are ye daft, Laddy? Of course, she... Well, I am not sure, Laddy! She did have on a ring...but that could have been for anything.

Are ye daft Paddy or just stupid? Quit worrying about me love life and would ye please quit playing Cupid!

January 15, 2022

The Luck of the Irish

"'Tis the season of hunting, me favorite time a year." Me bride said to "go take a break. Go have some fun, for goodness' sake! It would do ye no harm to go a hunting and get away from the farm."

So I packed up me groceries and all me gear. "Ah, I love this time o' year!" I kissed me bride and said goodbye; I was so excited that I could cry.

I could na' wait to get into the brush but told me self, "Take your time. There is no rush. Ah, I love this time o' year!"

For miles and miles did I drive, with hours to go afore I arrive. The excitement was so exhilarating. And that big old stag, he be just there awaiting. "Ah, I love this time o' year!"

I finally arrive at me camping site. It was getting dark and no longer light. I put up me tent and rolled out me bag. "In the morn, if the good Lord willin', I will have me stag!"

I awoke early in the morn. There was a hole in me tent. It looked to be torn. It could be nothing else; it was caused by a horn.

I be a peeking out of me tent and was so surprised. It was the stag that tore me tent, or so I surmised.

He was so huge, so majestic. He was quite an eyeful. As I turned, thinking, *Ye are mine!* It struck me that I left one thing behind, and it be not so trifle.

"You can be sure I will be back next year but will surely bring me rifle."

"Alas, I love this time o' year."

January 15, 2022

Holiday

"I have been tinking, Sven, ve need to go on holiday."

"But ver, Ole? Ve both like vorking so much, and ver is it ve vould be going? And ver vould ve stay?"

"Oh, I don't know for sure, Sven, but I tink ve should wisit Norvay."

"So vat do you tink? Vat do you have to say? Ole, I tink you have been drinking. I tink ve need to stay. Let's go back to verk and tink about dis anoter day."

"Oh, Sven, you are such a vorry vart. Ve vell be gone, and it vell be yust a short stay. So let's go, Sven. Let's be on our vay!"

"Ole, how much money is in your pocket?" "Vell right now not much, but I have my vatch and such, and I know ver I can hawk it!"

"Ole, I tink your brain is lame, and mine vould be da same if ve pursued these adwentures!"

"Ole, your vatch is vore out, and I am sure dey von't give you a ting for your dentures."

"Vell, it vas only a taught, Sven, and maybe all for naught, and I vas drinking my gin." "But how else can you plan a trip if you don't take a nip?"

"Vell, you can't even imagine!"

January 21, 2022

Why?

"My heart, my heart aches! It aches for the homeless. It aches for the poor. There are no particular races, just look at their faces. My heart aches to its core."

So many destitute, people asking for handouts. "There are a few. Their children in tears… They are the standouts."

"Why were they chosen to be the poor of this earth? I have so much guilt. Why was I chosen to have a gold-laced quilt?"

"Did I live in another time? Did I toil in dirt? Did I toil in grime? Did I earn my position in life? Why was I born to a rich man and wife?"

"Did I deserve my beautiful children and my place in this life?"

"Why was I blessed with all of these gifts? I have so many questions, but please, I don't need suggestions. All I need is one answer: Why?"

February 1, 2022

The Penitent

"I have angst, and I worry! What would it be like to be judged, to sit before a panel of my peers, being judged for my past and all those years?"

"Have I done enough in this life? Have I atoned enough for all my sins? Will all my I'm sorries suffice?"

"Have I done enough to show that I cared? Have I tried hard enough to make right all my wrongs?"

"Did I attend church enough and sing its songs? Did I try hard enough to make new friends? If I offended some, did I try to make amends? Did I talk behind their back? Did I do it because of something that I lack?"

"Did I judge people by their looks, just like covers on many books? Was I judged in another life? Was I single then, or did I have a wife?"

"Is this life I am living my sentence for all my past sins? I ask for forgiveness, and I do have remorse!"

"For in the end, after living my life, there is no recourse!"

"Was it enough? I have angst, and I worry!"

Marital Discord

"Laddy, I be having such bad news." "Oh! What would that be, Paddy?

"Me bride says she be a leaving me if I don't change me ways."

"Oh, I see, Paddy. Could it be the drinking? Is that what she be a thinking?"

"Are ye daft, Laddy? I only be a drinking during the weekday and maybe just one on Saturday, no more than two and nary a one on Sunday. Laddy, what I be saying be true!"

"Oh, I see, Paddy. Could it be the snoring?"

"Ye know, ye sound like a tugboat pulling into the mooring."

"Are ye daft, Laddy? If I be a snoring, she'd surely be kicking me out of bed by the morning!"

"Oh, I see, Paddy. Not to get into your personal life, but are ye respectful of your beautiful wife?"

"Are ye daft, Laddy? Of course, I be respectful! Although at times in the pub, when I get me an eyeful, it is me left eye that I rub. And now that you mention it, I'm a thinking, it be my left eye that goes a winking."

"Are ye daft, Paddy?"

February 11, 2022

Poems and Prose

"The beauty we see in life, such as a beautiful woman or a beautiful rose, is described to us in poems and prose."

"Does a rose know when it's being admired? Should you tell a woman that she is beautiful and that she is desired?"

Many people walk by a rose, never really smelling it or looking at it up close. They fail to see the beauty of its every petal, every petal of that beautiful rose. "It's described to us in poems and prose."

What determines the beauty of a woman? Is it her smile, the sparkle in her eyes? Or is it the aura that she presents? "It is described to us in poems and prose!"

"As she ages, her beauty will begin to wane, like the petals falling off that beautiful rose. She will resort to the memories of her youth, her beauty long gone, her legacy described to us in poems and prose."

"Enjoy your youth, my lovely rose! You will never be prettier or more desired!"

"This is described in poems and prose."

February 25, 2022

Man of the House

"Oh, Laddy, I have such bad news!" "Oh, what would that be, Paddy?" "It be such a sad situation, Laddy. Me lovely bride says a mouse is running rampant all through me house!"

"Oh, I see, Paddy. Have ye tried to catch it?" "Are ye daft, Laddy? Of course, I be trying to catch it, but me lovely bride be throwing a girly fit! She says to take charge and be a man. I be a trying, Laddy. I be giving it all that I can!"

"Oh, I see, Paddy, but have ye not tried a trap?"

"Are ye daft, Laddy?" Of course, I be trying a trap, and I be using cheese! But it ran in and out of that trap so fast and as pretty as you please!"

"Oh, I see, Paddy. Have you tried a cat?" "Are ye daft, Laddy? Of course I be trying a cat! I bought one from neighbor Fred. It be quite a mouser, or so he said."

"Oh, I see, Paddy. Did the cat catch the mouse?"

"Are ye daft, Laddy? That mouse chased the cat right out of me house!" "Oh, I see, Paddy. Then yer giving it up?" "Are ye daft, Laddy? I am thinking I have come to the conclusion that I will adopt that mouse and build him a house. That would be a good solution."

"Of course I be giving him a proper name, and me bride won't be the wiser when I surprise her and surely will think it be tame…" "Are ye daft, Paddy?"

February 26, 2022

The Creep of Socialism

"Yesterday is gone. Tomorrow is yond."

"Every moment of every day is a gift. Moments given… Moments taken. Hearts are broken, some forsaken"

"Maybe it will change…maybe tomorrow!"

"The gift of life so often forlorn, many given up, as though never born." Discarded by some, "given no chance to prove their worth, hated from the moment…the moment of their birth."

"Maybe it will change…maybe tomorrow! The morals taught to our children for more than a generation with little thought for their parents' veneration. Taking our children from us, little by little, a day at a time, in such small increments, we would see no crime."

"Maybe it will change…maybe tomorrow! I cry as I search for the truth, knowing full well they are stealing our youths, turning them against the values we hold dear, a little bit more year by year."

"Maybe it will change…maybe tomorrow! Our faiths are shaken, but we are not mistaken. There is only today. There is no tomorrow, for tomorrow turns into today. Something needs to be done today, not tomorrow!"

"Let us pray!"

April 11, 2022

Regrets

What am I doing? Just sitting here, drinking an ice-cold beer, thinking of all my failures in life, wishing you were here, wishing you were still my wife.

Honey, how long has it been? Sure would like to see you. Sure would like to see you again!

Ya, I know! You begged me to change my ways. I didn't listen, now I'm sitting here, wondering who you're kissing.

Honey, does he look into your beautiful blue eyes? Does he run his fingers through your silky brown hair?

Honey, does he wrap his arms around you like I used to do? Does he let his love surround you?

Honey, how long has it been? Sure would like to see you. Sure would like to see you again!

Honey, does he love to smell your perfume that's in your hair?

If only I had listened, maybe I'd still be there. Oh, how I miss seeing your beautiful face when you woke up every morning. I had my chance you gave me fair warning.

Honey, how long has it been? Sure would like to see you! Sure would like to see you again!

Sometimes I wonder if maybe I would still be there. If only I wouldn't have drunk all that beer, maybe fulfilling more of your dreams.

I guess I'm just a born loser, or so it seems.

Honey, how long has it been? Sure would like to see you! Sure would like to see you again!

You didn't deserve the way I treated you. You know, every girl I went home with was just something new, but in the morning, she just wasn't you.

Honey, when I came home, I'd be crying, trying not to wake you, trying not to make a sound, knowing that I failed you again, knowing that I let you down!

Honey, how long has it been? Sure would like to see you. Sure would like to see you again.

Honey, I just want you to know, your love for me was as good as it gets!

Goodbye, honey, I'm going to crack open another ice-cold beer and face the day alone again, thinking of you, honey, and all my regrets.

April 22, 2022

I'm Done Talking

I came home from work and asked my son, Where's your mom? He said, She's out again, Dad.

I said, son, this isn't good, but I'm not surprised. You see, son, when she comes home late at night, she always starts lying to make it right.

It's just one more thing that makes our rings worthless things.

Son, I just want to make it clear. I've tried, and I've tried. I've cried, and I've cried... I'm done talking.

I got down on my knees. I begged her pretty please. I'm done talking. I'm walking. I'm walking right out of here!

Son, I always knew when she was lying. She couldn't look me in the eyes without crying.

Son, I know she could see what she was doing to me. I'm pretty sure she doesn't want me here.

Son, I just want to make it clear. I've tried. and I've tried. I've cried. and I've cried... I'm done talking! I got down on my knees. I begged her pretty please. I'm done talking. I'm walking. I'm walking right out of here.

Son, I know there was a time she cared about all the things we shared.

When did she stop loving me? What did I do? Where did I go wrong? Was she doing this all along?

Thinking back, I can't remember the last time she said I love you.

Son, I just want to make it clear. I've tried, and I've tried. I've cried, and I've cried. I'm done talking.

I got down on my knees and begged her pretty please. I'm done talking, I'm walking, I'm walking right out of here.

Son, it's true. I didn't father you, but I've loved you as my own from day one.

I'm so sorry this is how it ended. It's not your fault, and it's not what I intended.

Son, I did all I could. I did all I could do. My only regret, son, I won't have you.

Let me make it clear. I tried, and I tried, cried, and I cried. I'm done talking. I got down on my knees. I begged her pretty please. I'm done talking. I'm walking. I'm walking right out of here.

Son, my only regret is I won't have you.

Johnny No Name... Rock Star?

From the time I was young, I loved to listen to the rock stars sing. They weren't that good. But listen up! Here's the thing! You didn't have to be real good. Just put on a good show, smile at all the beautiful women, and wink at all the pretty young girls.

You know I couldn't even sing! How could you go wrong? Every night, a new gig, a new girl…beer, whiskey, and song!

I thought I was so cool, everything going my way. Party all night, sleep all day.

I played in town after town, gig after gig! My popularity soaring, my head getting so big!

I hit the big time. I could do no wrong! Every night a new gig, a new girl…beer, whiskey, and song!

I knew my time was short and coming to an end. I was getting tired and growing old. Most all my records were hits, many solid golds!

I bought a big house, a beautiful yacht, a new jet! If I didn't have it, it was only because I hadn't thought of it yet.

I threw parties that entertained me for days. If I grew bored, I would always find new ways!

Then in a blink of an eye, it was all over; I was a has-been. I couldn't even draw a small group of friends, little lone a crowd! I couldn't admit it; I was just too proud.

I had nothing to show for my success except for a few hit records, many of them gold.

I didn't even save a dime! But one thing is for sure! I wouldn't change a thing. I had one helluva good time! A new gig a new girl… beer, whiskey, and song!

Now listen up. Here's the thing: I wasn't real good, but I did put on a good show. I smiled at all the women and winked at all the pretty girls… I didn't do too bad for a guy who couldn't sing.

July 20, 2022

Paddy Waxes Poetic?

Laddy, I be so sad! I don't know what to do! Why would that be, Paddy? Laddy, it be my lovely bride. She be thinking I do not love her, and I be just taking her in stride!

Paddy! Why would that be? Laddy, me lovely bride is telling me that all of her girly mates be getting a poem from their mates! Laddy, I say that is a bunch of blarney! They are just funning with her and don't even show 'em!

Paddy! Have ye given her gifts? Are ye daft, Laddy? For sure I be giving her gifts!—necklaces, rings and all kinds of fun things, although maybe some from the local pawn.

Laddy, me lovely bride be saying she will not be happy till she gets her poem. And it's to be a beauty, so she can show 'em!

Laddy! She be saying it has to come from me heart! For sure I be not knowing the words or even where to start.

Paddy! Why can't ye be just telling her how ye feel? Are ye daft, Laddy? Ye need to be a writing the words, and for sure, they better be for real!

Paddy! Have ye whispered sweet nothings in her ear when alone in the bed, and she be in the loving way?

Are ye daft, Laddy? Every night and every day! I be giving her a peck on the cheek and a pat on her bottom! And then I be reminding her of all me gifts and the reason that she got 'em!

Paddy! What will ye do then? Laddy! After a great deal of thought, I have decided to go to the Walmart and buy a card, maybe even a Hallmark.

I know it will be their words, Laddy. But even at that, they will be from me own heart. I will copy them, and she will be none the wiser! Maybe not a perfect solution but certainly a good start. And besides, I can't think of anything better to surprise her.

Are ye daft, Paddy?

August 4, 2022

The Devil's Sweat!

Whiskey! Here's to you, my friend! You never let me down! Some people call it the devil's sweat. I would be willing to bet that I'm not done with our relationship, not quite yet!

We have become good friends, you and me! When I get lonesome, I pour me a shot and say here's to you, my friend! I guess it's you and me. You're all that I've got!

There is nobody around telling me I need to slow down! It's just you and me, my friend, nobody else here, not a peep, not a sound!

You would be surprised at all the feelings hidden and all the feelings that are disguised!

All the many thoughts that go through my head and all the many thoughts that I have surmised!

Have another shot, my friend. Today is all but done! Your life full of misery, and sorrow has only just begun!

It's going to be a short life, you can be sure, because the life that I'm living is no answer, and it's certainly no cure!

I think eventually I will be rid of you…but not quite just yet!

August 12, 2022

Paddy Goes Shopping

Oh, Laddy! It is trouble I be havin'! Oh! And what would that be, Paddy? Well, as ye well know, it is a hardworking man that I am, and ye well know, no man works harder!

Well, me lovely bride sent me to the market to pick up some groceries and what not, to restock the larder. Paddy! Did ye get the groceries and what not? Are ye daft, Laddy? What kind of husband would I be if I be not doing what she be asking of me?

So, Paddy! Why is it trouble ye be havin'? Ye did as she asked and went right home shortly after. Are ye daft, Laddy? Why of course, I…well, I did stop at Gilley's Pub for a pint of ale and some laughter! And, Laddy, ye well know the hardworking man that I am. It was just to be one and go home to me lovely bride shortly thereafter!

Paddy, did ye go on home shortly thereafter? Are ye daft, Laddy? Of course I be going home shortly thereafter! Laddy, I only had the one, mind you! No more than two! And for sure, no more than three! But now, Laddy, as ye well know, me memory does fail me from time to time! No, Laddy, it was three that I be havin'. Well…no more than four for sure!

Paddy! Did ye then go home? Are ye daft, Laddy? Of course I be going home! Although, I did sit on the bread, and all the frozen goods had went to thaw. Laddy, I knew I was in trouble beyond a doubt! Ye never heard the likes of a women to scream louder. And, oh, can she shout!

Paddy, did ye say ye were sorry? Are ye daft, Laddy? Of course I be saying I'm sorry!

But she just stomped off to bed and yelled that I had better figure it out! Paddy, did ye figure it out? Are ye daft, Laddy? Of course
I figured it out!

I went back to Gilley's Pub and had a couple more pints. Now
mind you, Laddy, I only had two and no more than three!

Ye know, Laddy, as I sat there with a clear head, I decided, from
this day forward, I will stop at Gilley's Pub first, and then there will
be no more of the frozen food going to thaw, and there will be no
more of me sitting on the bread!

Are ye daft, Paddy?

August 13, 2022

Here's to You!

Ah! It's a good shot of Irish whiskey I be havin'! Just the thing to make me feel patriotic and let freedom ring! Here's to you, America!

Would you join me in one down the chute? Nothing works better to make you more patriotic or more resolute!

I salute you, Stars and Stripes! There is no place on earth where they have so much freedom and yet so many gripes!

Here is another shot, and it's to you! Be humble, and be kind to others! And maybe they will be kind to you!

Have no hate nor animosity! Be kind to others; show them your love! Show them true generosity!

Offer them a chair, for they may have been traveling a while. Offer them your hand, and don't forget to smile!

This country has so much vitriol and hate; you could have been one of them if not for fate.

It could have been you who needed that chair. Come on! Be truthful! Be honest! Be fair!

Have another shot! Here's to you! Go ahead, admit it! You didn't earn your right to be here. It was just the luck of the draw. It was a gift to you! You say don't come to my state! Don't come to my city.

Here's another shot to you, and here's another for your pomposity! This is America of thee I sing! It's still a free country… Let freedom ring! This country so beautiful, so regal! Please open your arms! Let's just make sure they are legal!

August 20, 2022

Be Leery of Leprechauns Gifts!

Laddy! The most amazing thing happened to me last eve at Gilley's Pub! Ye will not believe your ears! Oh! What would that be, Paddy?

Well, Laddy! Ye know I be a hardworking man and need to stop at the pub once in a while! You know! Just to relax!

Oh! So ye stopped at the pub just to relax, and ye din' have an ale? Are ye daft, Laddy?

Of course I be having an ale but only one! Well, maybe two! But no more than three for certain!

So, Paddy! What was so amazing? Now, Laddy, I be getting to it! It be something real, or it be ridicule I be facing! Oh! So ye went right home? Are ye daft, Laddy? No! I didn't go right home!

Now, Laddy, be quiet and don't tell a soul! I seen me a leprechaun! He was hiding at the end of the bar! He went, Psst! Psst! Down here!

When I looked down, I could na believe me eyes! Laddy, when I looked down, there he was! Just a tiny little thing! No bigger than me leg. I looked around and made no sound, for I didn't know what he wanted of me.

Paddy! How many ales did ye have? Are ye daft, Laddy? I told ye it was three! Well, maybe four, but, Laddy, for sure not more than five!

Laddy, he said to bend over so he could whisper in me ear. He said he lived in a tree in the dale and would grant me one wish if I would buy him a pint of ale.

Paddy, what was the wish that he be promising ye? Are ye daft, Laddy? He said, if I be telling a soul, it would na come true!

So, Paddy, ye bought him an ale? Are ye daft, Laddy? Of course I be buying him an ale! Well maybe two and no more than three!

Paddy! When will he be making your wish come true? Well, now, Laddy, this is the best part! He said to come to the biggest tree in the dale. There I would be having me wishes unfold, or I could have a choice of a great, big pot of gold!

Paddy! Did ye go to the biggest tree in the dale? Are ye daft, Laddy? Of course I went to the biggest tree in the dale!

Well, Paddy? Well, Laddy! He left me a note, telling me to meet him at the pub, and it was a generous offer he proposed.

He said he would double me wishes with a gift for the misses but only if we stayed until it closed!

Are ye daft, Paddy?

Lady of the Evening

When women discovered red paint to color their lips and figured out how to swing those hips and splash that perfume all over the place, and, oh, those stockings made of black nylon and pretty black lace!

That black eyeliner around their eyes, oh! How that made them sparkle and surely mesmerize! But it was all over boys when they mastered that wink! It definitely proved that we were the missing link!

It didn't take long once they caught your eye! You would do anything they wanted, and that's no lie! Anything they asked, you would do it, and you didn't even know why!

Oh! Those pretty red lips and those swinging hips, they have roped a cowboy or two, but you knew they weren't near as handsome and surely weren't as cute as you!

There are some reasons for all that teasing and all that winking! There is no turning back once your hooked… You just stand there with your tongue hanging out and your eyes a blinking!

Your Adam's apple a bouncing, like you're dying of thirst! Your body not knowing whether it's coming or going or which one would be worst!

Throughout history, the story is the same. She said I have the most beautiful blue eyes she had ever seen! That should have been my first clue… My eyes aren't blue; they are green!

She said, Would you mind buying me a drink? You handsome young man! Of course I stayed, but I should have ran!

Those pretty red lips and those swinging hips, they had me from the start! But it's not what you think! She knew she had me hooked…when she gave me that wink!

She asked, Would you like to cut cards to see who buys the next round? It sounded good to me, and the reasoning was sound.

The more I got to drinking, the more I got to thinking… I don't think I even won one draw! There was something funny, for I had no more money, and I think it went down her bra!

Oh! Those red lips and those swinging hips, and it's not what you think! Once it began, I surely had fun. And when she departed, I know it was good-hearted because she said goodbye with a wink!

October 16, 2022

A Loved One Lost

The past is gone, leaving us alone to look forward to what is beyond!

We have been left alone for a reason! We know not for how long, maybe for months or maybe just a season!

We face the finality and start to realize, this is our lives now; this is our new reality.

As we spend this time to heal from all the twists and all the turns, all of the pains and the hurt we felt, it's time to move forward! It's time to play the cards that we were dealt!

Most will make it through this time, having their memories and still do cry. Others will let it go without a second thought! They will move forward without so much as a blink of an eye.

Nonetheless, this is our new lives. It is now up to us to put up the gallant fight, never knowing when it is our turn, when our end will be, never seeing the end in sight... And we wait!

October 16, 2022

Weight and Worry

Scientists are deducing that we should be reducing. Oh, how brilliant they are!

When you start looking, it doesn't matter who's cooking, all you see is sugar and carbs and the FDA pointing fingers. And their thoughts, they do linger. Their advice not so much helpful but barbs!

They tell us to eat this and tell us to eat that! It's too high in this and too high in that. Besides, it's so full of fat!

When you follow their advice (by the way, how is that working for you?), don't surmise!

I know what you're thinking, but your clothes are not shrinking! The truth is, you just need a larger size!

For what it's worth, we have exploded our girth. Our bodies are wrecks. But, oh, what the heck. We can just buy new clothes made of polyester and spandex.

When I weigh, it shows I've gained five pounds! You've got to be joking! Of course, it's the scale! It must be broken!

When I look at my thighs, all I see are burgers and fries! And that belly…peanut butter and jelly! That double chin! When did that begin?

Oh, what the hay! Tomorrow's another day. And besides, I've got a cure, and that's for sure! I have seen a new ad for a new diet! It's the latest craze. I think I will try it! It says, if you follow the directions for thirty days, they guarantee your weight and your worries will be behind you! Hmm? Imagine that!

November 24, 2022

Lost in Heartache... a Prayer

I visit the edge of heaven. I go there quietly almost every day. I cannot get in yet, but that's where I kneel, and that's where I pray. I share my heartache with the angels!

Sometimes it's so quiet there as I begin to pray, and sometimes... sometimes I hear them! I hear the angels. I don't understand what they are saying, but maybe, just maybe, it might be my time! It might be my turn! Maybe they have come for me. Maybe this is my day! But slowly...very slowly, I hear their voices growing softer, like clouds drifting away. I will return tomorrow to my edge of heaven, and I will kneel, and I will pray and maybe tomorrow, if not surely another day!

I know they can hear me; they can hear the words that I pray! I kneel and get down on my knees and pray... Please! Please! Hear my prayer! Let it not be tomorrow, but please... Please!

Let it be today!
Amen!

November 28, 2022

A Love Story

Honey! Do you remember when you were little? How I held you, and Mom and I shared our bed, with you in the middle? We wanted to show you how much we loved you and how much we cared!

What happened? I did everything I could for Mom and for you from day one! She had my heart the day I met her! I made a vow I would love her until death do us part! Where did I go wrong? What did I do? I loved her with all of my heart!

She was my everything, and I loved her with everything I had right from the start! I don't know what happened; we were one for so many years!

What happened to our love, sis? There are so many things gone wrong, but the love is what I miss! Everything else is just a sad song!

Please, sis! Tell me where I went wrong! When did she give up on me? How do I ask for forgiveness from somebody gone? Sis! Where did I go wrong?

I was working hard hours! Sometimes miserable! Sometimes long!

I want to forgive her for some things she did! I want to forgive her for something she hid!

It wasn't me, sis! Although I did wrong! It takes two to make a marriage and to make it strong!

Where did I go wrong? How do I live with this? How do I live with this?

January 21, 2023

An Old-Timer's Dilemma

Twill it will, or twill it won't? It is but a question, but it be my question, if I do or if I don't! But if I do, and maybe I won't!

Don't disparage me! Please! Please don't!

I need to ponder over this question. Twill I will, or twill I won't! Should I stand up, or should I sit down? How do I do it wearing this damned gown?

It be but a question. Which would work for me? Which would be best? When will I go home? I am sure I am here as a guest!

I am lost in a sea of questions. Should I, or should I not? Finding the answers be so complex, it be not so easy! So many questions!

Twill I will, or twill I won't? What will happen if I do or maybe if I don't? I think the answer is the right one, and it be the one I choose!

Oh, how I long for a shot of good Irish whiskey; that would surely refresh me mind! But believe me, I have looked far and wide, and there is not a drop that was left behind!

I know I be choosing a proper answer, and I be quite sure what it was but a new problem has arose. I simply can't remember me question as I be looking at the John, trying to remember the answer to the one that I chose!

I think that I will go pee, and maybe me memory will come back to me.

Time will tell, and maybe... What was it I was going to say?

Alas! Twill it will, or twill it won't

February 10, 2023

Paddy Is Going Sober?

Laddy! I be having such good news! Oh! What would that be, Paddy? Laddy, I have decided to change me ways! Oh, and how would that be, Paddy? I have decided it's time to quit me drinking, and I have decided, Laddy, that I could wear sobriety on me face. But ye know, Laddy, forever be a long, long time. It's more than just a couple of days!

Paddy! Can I be of any help? Are ye daft, Laddy? What would be lovely bride be thinking if I had to ask for help to quit me drinking?

Oh! I see, Paddy! So this is something ye are thinking of doing but not quite yet?

Are ye daft, Laddy? Of course, I be ready to quit me drinking! But this be not an easy chore.

I really need to consider this and think about it more. Oh! I see, Paddy. Is this something that your lovely bride has maybe suggested?

Are ye daft, Laddy? Why, Laddy, this be something I be thinking on me own… Well, she did maybe make a wee suggestion! Oh! What would that be, Paddy? Well now, Laddy, it was no big blowup, but she did mention, if I didn't, coming home would be out of the question! Oh! I see, Paddy. So are ye quitting?

Are ye daft, Laddy? Well now, there is a lot to ponder. So I think I will go down to the pub Gilley. Ye know, the one down yonder? I wouldn't want to be doing anything rash. Besides, I hear they are having a big bash.

Now, Laddy, I be having but one pint and no more than two and certainly no more than three!

Anyways, ye know I cannot quit me drinking all at once. And, Laddy, tonight you buy two pints, and the third one is free!

Are ye daft, Paddy?

February 12, 2023

Just Wanted You to Know

Darlin', you've been gone now for a while, and I don't really know where to start, looking back and remembering all the years we shared, all our ups and downs, all the smiles, and all the frowns.

We had so many good years together, but we sure had some bad! And it wasn't just that, look at all that we had.

Darlin', I just want you to know, I always loved you, and you always had my heart!

There were days I'm sure you doubted my love for you, and you probably had good reason. But I want you to know, you were my shining light when I got lost. You were always there; you were my beacon.

Darlin', I just want you to know, I always loved you, and you always had my heart!

I don't know why I ever cheated, because you had it all, everything I loved and everything I needed. You were the reason our marriage lasted and the reason our marriage succeeded!

Darlin', I just want you to know, I always loved you, and you always had my heart!

I know I wasn't a good husband or a good dad to the children that I fathered, and I have often wondered why you stayed with me, why you even bothered!

Darlin', I just want you to know, I always loved you, and you always had my heart!

Many years have passed since I lost you; it seems like just yesterday. Why didn't I pay more attention to you and maybe listen to more of what you had to say? I could have changed so many things. I could have bought you more flowers! I could have bought you diamond rings! I could have changed. I could have changed so many things.

Darlin', I just want you to know, I always loved you, and you always had my heart!

Hindsight is an unforgiving and cruel teacher. It's not a friend, and I will live with my regrets until the bitter end!

Darlin', I just want you to know, I always loved you, and you always had my heart! You always had my heart!

February 15, 2023

Valentine's Day Wish

Another Valentine's Day we put in the past. My goodness, another year—where did time go? It went so fast!

Although I didn't get any flowers or boxes of chocolate and for certain a card saying be mine, and nobody asked me, How are you doing? Well, just to let you know, I am doing just fine.

Cupid took a shot at my heart, but it did not break as his shot hit low, hence my love for steak.

I hope your day was filled with hugs and kisses, and I wish you a blessed day, whether it be mister or missus.

February 26, 2023

Wee Winking Willie

There once was a good old lad named Wee Winking Willie. He spent his time at the local pub called Gilley. He wasn't very tall. And when he be drinking, he said, "It not be mattering what ye be thinking." And upon seeing all the pretty lassies, he would tip his hat and smile. And with a jump in the air, a click of his heels, and his eye would go a winking.

Some lassies would surely be winking back at Willie, although they didn't quite know what he be a thinking, agreed that he became quite silly when he be a drinking.

He could whistle a tune to any occasion; it be not mattering where or what the location! And after another drink, he would sing "Rattlin' Roaring Willie." It was that tune I'm pretty sure…at least I be a thinking! And with a tip of the hat and a smile, a jump in the air, a click of his heels, his eye would go a winking. He would say, "Bar woman, give me another ale! For I be not done with me drinking!"

He grabbed her hand and gave her a twirl and kissed her on her… Well, if she be shorter, it would have been the neck! She slapped his face and said, "I be not that kind of lass. And just to let you know, Willie, that drink will be your last."

With the tip of his hat, a smile, a jump in the air, a click of his heels, and his eye a winking, he said, "I will see you tomorrow, same time. I be a thinking!" As he went out the door, he looked back, and not saying a word, with a smile on her face, she was there; she was there just a winking!

About the Author

Michael Beebe Sr. was born in Longview, Washington, in 1947.

Michael attended local schools and graduated from R.A. Long High School in 1965.

Michael enlisted in the US Air Force in 1966, serving as a dental tech and, in 1968, married the love of his life, Michele Peret. Upon being discharged from the service in 1969, Michael and wife, Michele, returned to Longview for a short time, moving to Castle Rock ten miles north of Longview in 1969. Michael also started working as an industrial firefighter for International Paper Company that same year. During their stay in Castle Rock (fourteen years), they began also raising their children, Shelley and Michael Jr.

In 1979, wanting something different, Michael became a union carpenter for a short time, working on building North Bonneville Dam and power station. A short time later, Michael worked for Ross Simmons Hardwoods as a carpenter, dry kiln, and boiler operator, as well as planer setup man. Michael stayed there until 1984 when the family moved back to Longview and accepted a position in shipping at Longview Fibre (pulp and paper mill), where Michael worked and medically retired in 2006 after twenty-two years.

Upon retiring, Michael and Michele RV'd for several years, making many friends. In 2018, Michael sold his motor home as he could no longer physically maintain it.

Michael's wife, Michele, was diagnosed on April 2, 2020, with terminal bile duct cancer and passed away on April 22, 2020. Michael was devastated and emotionally destroyed.

Michael started going to a therapy session at a hospice, and it was there that a counselor suggested he try writing poetry about his loss and to date each one so he would see his progression from heartache to happiness.

Michael didn't immediately start writing until February 2021, when he moved to Gold Canyon, Arizona, having written a short thank-you poem to the previous owners who threw him a welcome party the night before he moved in, and that started a late-in-life love of writing poetry.

Michael had no intentions of publishing his poems, but they helped him so much with handling and dealing with his emotions; Michael thought maybe his writings would help others heal.

Michael wants to emphasize that healing doesn't happen overnight, but heal you will!

Michael will always have a place in his heart for his wife, Michele!

I hope you will enjoy his book as well as your journey to healing. You will laugh again!

Printed in the USA
CPSIA information can be obtained
at www.ICGtesting.com
CBHW051117081124
17082CB00021B/559

9 798893 093759